Book
for
Oreo

Caralee A. Jardine

Dedication

In loving memory of Oreo Jardine, I dedicate this book to all the pets and wildlife that lost their lives in the Fort McMurray wild fires of 2016.

This book will be used to start a foundation in Oreo's memory and to raise funds for various animal charities.

Tellwell Talent
www.tellwell.ca

ISBN
978-1-77302-201-7 (Paperback)
978-1-77302-202-4 (eBook)

"Watch the animals they will teach you…."
Job12:7

Table of Contents

Prelude

As a young girl I had one dream…to be a wife and a mother. By the time I was 21 I was dating the love of my life, my soul mate. After years of dating we started growing apart due to our individual relationships with God. I sensed God was asking me to surrender him, and I fought with God for six months prior to ending my relationship with the man I loved more than life itself.

I believed this man would eventually rededicate his life to God and we would get married after all. Unfortunately for me he ended up marrying someone else. I accused God of lying to me and ended up turning my life upside down and inside out to the point where it was hardly even recognizable.

My dreams of being a wife and a mother crashed down all around me. As I struggled to understand God's purpose he used my cat, Oreo, to show me he had indeed blessed me with a great gift. A gift of singleness and of motherhood.

He blessed me with a son. A son who walked on four legs instead of two and had fur instead of hair, but a son in every way. A son that would never talk back to me, or try my patience. A son that would not grow into a rebellious teen, or graduate from high school/ college and move away. A son who would always be there to comfort me and love me unconditionally. A son that would provide so much fun and joy and became my biggest fan. A son who would fill the hole that was yearning for a husband and children. A son that would show me how much God loved me and lead me back to God.

This book was written to honor his memory and his life. When I began writing the purpose was simply to honor my commitment to Oreo. Upon completing Oreo's book I feel God is asking me to have it published so others may also find encouragement through Oreo's life. The pages in it are based on actual events and our remarkable journey together as mother and son.

You don't know love, till you've known the love of a cat.

Chapter 1

Adoption

It all started by getting a phone call from my sister- in- law Glenda. She was going to the Calgary Humane Society to look for a puppy and wanted me to come along. We arrived at the Humane Society that Saturday afternoon and saw so many loveable dogs and puppies, just not one that was right for Glenda. On our way out of the dog kennels, I looked at Glenda and said, "Let's stop and see the kitties." I always had a dog and two cats growing up, so I couldn't pass by the cat kennels without giving them a little love.

I had just moved into an apartment that was in the process of changing their pet rule. Current owners could have pets, new tenants could not. I had just moved in a couple months earlier and knew I wasn't allowed to have a pet, but I wanted to see the kitties anyway. There were so many cats and kittens. There was a big orange tabby that looked like my previous cat Leopard and a grey and white one that reminded me of Misty. I glanced at all the cats, petting each one as I continued walking through out the room. All of a sudden this tiny white paw shot out of a cage and grabbed my arm; his claws clung to my jacket as he pulled me closer to his cage. Both Glenda and I were stunned. "I can't believe it" Glenda exclaimed "He picked you!" As I released his claws from my jacket I opened his cage, and held the six month old kitten. He nestled into my chest and rubbed his head on my chin, begging me to take him home. After a few minutes I couldn't resist so I memorized the information on his card…Oreo, approx. d.o.b. May 1'2000, six months old, black and white DSH. I opened his cage and put Oreo back in. He looked so sad and heartbroken as he watched me walk away.

I proceeded to the adoption desk and filled out all the paperwork to start the adoption process. The women behind the desk took my form and called my landlord to ask if I was allowed to have a pet in my suite. My landlord said no, and that was that, or so I thought.

I got home that night and as I tried to sleep I dreamt of this little kitty that desperately needed a home. I dreamt of his tiny little paw shooting out of the cage, begging me to take him home, looking so sad as I walked away. "I'm sorry Oreo, I tried but the apartment said no", I cried in my sleep. Needless to say it was a very restless sleep, with this tiny kitten tugging at my heart strings. Little did I know this was only the beginning of many nights, Oreo calling "I need you" as I slept.

Every night after my visit to the Humane Society I dreamt of this little kitten. Finally as I left work on Wednesday October 18' 2000, I knew Oreo was destined to be mine. I had to find a way of rescuing him. I started driving to the Humane Society and I called my aunt Natalie. Natalie was always someone I could always count on and I thought of her more as a big sister than an aunt. I told Natalie about this six month old kitten that has had a rough start to life. He had been abused and someone had tried to neuter him themselves so his back end was a little messed up. I told her how he picked me with his paw shooting out of his cage, but the apartment said no. She said

"You have to get that cat, He is your kitty. How can I help?" Natalie and I talked for a bit and made our plan.

As soon as I got off the phone with Natalie I called the Humane Society. I told them I was on my way to adopt Oreo. It was almost 5pm and I was stopped at a red light only minutes away. The female voice on the other end of the line told me I had better hurry since it's almost closing time and he won't be here at eight in the morning. I knew that meant he was scheduled to be euthanized as they only kept cats for ten days. This was his tenth day. I got to the Humane Society with minutes to spare and rushed straight to the adoption desk. I redid all the paperwork, but this time I used my parents address with my aunt's phone number.

The woman behind the desk proceeded to call my aunt who pretended to be my mom. They asked why I had a different address since I had tried to adopt Oreo only a few days before. Natalie told them since they wouldn't allow me to have a cat, I moved back home so I could.

When the young woman came back to the desk I was anxiously waiting at, she handed me a box with little breathing holes. He's mine! I was so excited I rushed into the kennel room and straight to his cage. He wasn't in his cage! I started to panic as I thought "It's now after 5 pm and he's not in his cage." My heart sank. I instantly panic and call for Oreo. As I'm just starting to run out of the room to get help, I hear this faint meow from the corner of the room. There he is, in a little girls lap. I was so relieved to see him alive and well, I scooped him out of the little girls lap, put him in his box and drove home.

When I got home I realized I never said a word to the little girl, just grabbed my cat and left. "Oops", I thought, as I snuck up the stairwell of the apartment with my new kitten. I made it to my suite without being caught, and let Oreo out to roam his new home. He was so happy to have a home and be out of that cage.

As I watched him go room to room, I remembered them telling me he will probably find a place to hide for the first week and not to be surprised when I don't see him during that time. He continued roaming the apartment, while I reflected on the events of the last few days. He picked me with his paw shooting out of his cage, and looked so sad as I walked away. When I went back for him, it's like he sensed I was there for him. Here he was in the lap of this little girl, but when I called for him he answered, and was trying to get out of her lap and into my arms. It's almost like he knew I would be back for him. It's like he knew, I was his.

I hopped into bed that night praying that the apartment would let me keep this kitty. Knowing I had lied and that was not God's way of doing things. I prayed that Oreo would not be taken away from me knowing it was a possibility since I broke my rental contract.

As I was just starting to doze off this little ball of fur jumped into my bed and climbed under the covers, nestled into my chest and curled up under my arm. This was only the beginning of our insepa-rable bond.

Chapter 2

Mother's Day

Oreo mapped out our routine starting day one. I awoke to him bathing me with his tongue. He gently combed my hair with his claws as he licked the strands of my hair. When I tried to go back to sleep, he gently tapped my mouth with his paw. "Wake up, let's play" he'd say as I'd slowly make my way out of bed.

Our mornings were full of cuddles and purrs. Everywhere I went this little black and white fur ball would be at my heel. Even potty breaks were no longer private. He would jump into my lap anytime I sat down. When I hopped in the shower Oreo would be at the back of the tub playing with the water. As I'd shower with him playing, I sang to him. I made up songs for Oreo as we played and he loved his own songs. I always started with the first one which was to the tune of B.i.n.g.o.

"There is a girl named Caralee who has a precious kitty, O.R.E.O, O.R.E.O, O.R.E.O and Oreo is his name O."

Without missing a beat I'd start singing him his other song.

"There is a little kitty his name is Oreo and Oreo loves to play a game called hide and seek. Oh Oreo, Oreo how he loves to play, in a box, in a cupboard, underneath the bed, It doesn't really matter where, as long as he is hid. Oh Oreo, Oreo how he loves to play, and his favorite game of all is a game called hide and seek."

I knew instantly Oreo was special and not a typical cat. He was extremely loyal and affectionate. He acted more like a dog than a cat. So I decided to try to train him. I bought a collar, a leash and some treats. Oreo loved treats, especially if he got to eat them out of my hand.

I was amazed how quickly he learned to sit, lie down and beg on command. I worked with him patiently and lovingly an hour each day as he learned to accept the leash. I rewarded him with treats at every stage of him learning to walk around the apartment on the leash.

By the time spring rolled around Oreo was trained. I took him for walks around the apartment complex, took him to work and even camping at our family property. Everywhere I went Oreo was happy to tag along.

Our first Mother's day came and I couldn't imagine spending it without Oreo. So after brunch with my parents, brother and his wife, we decided to go for a walk around McKenzie Lake. I rushed home to get Orco, Cory and Glenda rushed home to get Shylo, the shiatzu puppy they adopted weeks after I got Oreo. When we arrived at my parent's house, Mom pronounces "My friends have grandkids, not me I have a grand cat and a grand dog." As we chuckled at how Oreo and Shylo have become more than just pets and are truly members of our family, we made our way to the bike path.

Oreo and Shylo proudly strutted along the path. Oreo loved all the attention he received. The more people laughed at the sight of a cat on a leash, the more he strutted. Oreo never believed he was a cat; he was convinced he was human and he certainly behaved more like a dog than a cat.

He loved showing off, and as we continued down the path he would stop to smell every flower and weed and nibble on the grass. Oreo liked to take his time, he wanted to breathe it all in. Shylo wanted to run. As Glenda tugged on Shylo's leash to slow her down, I tugged on Oreo's to speed him up. Shylo would turn back and look at Oreo and bark as if to say "Come on you slow poke, hurry up your slowing me down!" Oreo didn't care. The more I tugged on his leash the more determined he was to slow down. Grandpa (my dad) laughed at Oreo and all his stall tactics, so he nicknamed him "Mop."

We were just coming around a corner on the path, when I saw a German Shepard heading our way. "Oreo danger!" I exclaimed. Oreo sat down and waited for me to pick him up. I picked up Oreo and waited till the dog's owner shortened his leash before I passed by. Oreo calmly stayed in my arm's without scratching as we walked by the dog. Since we had fallen behind the others I continued down the path with Oreo in my arms.

When we finally caught up with them it was time to go home. Oreo walked all the way back to my parent's house and climbed into my car. He was tired and slept all the way home, dreaming of the fun we had.

The apartment would get quite hot in the summer, and Oreo was constantly looking for ways to cool down. He'd sit at the open window in the kitchen and take in the cool breeze. When I'd go out on the balcony Oreo loved coming out too. I was nervous that he might jump off since we lived on the eighth floor, so I tied his leash to one of his heavier toys. We would spend our evenings on the balcony. Oreo loved the feel of the cool cement on his belly.

One afternoon I couldn't find Oreo. I was starting to panic since he was always at my heel. I was calling his name as I searched for him. I checked every cupboard, drawer and closets to no avail. Finally I heard banging. It was coming from the kitchen. I ran to the kitchen and heard the fridge rattle, I opened the door and out came Oreo. My cooled down kitty must have climbed into the fridge when I grabbed out my pop, moments before I noticed he was missing. The silly boy was so hot he was panting and needed somewhere cool. "Oops" I thought, "I guess I need to learn to double check every drawer, cupboard and fridge before I close it." It became a natural instinct to always check for Oreo before I open or close any kind of door.

Since the apartment was so hot, I was constantly looking for ways to cool Oreo down. He loved car rides, so on really hot days I'd take him in the car with the air conditioner blowing. I'd drive across the city with him on my lap, and he'd stick his nose out the window breathing in all the fresh air he could.

Since he loved car rides and did so well on his leash, I decided to escape the hot apartment for a weekend and take him camping at the family property in Rimbey. I placed his litter box on the floor under the back seats and away we went. It should only be a two hour drive, but Oreo needed a few bathroom breaks. After a few extra stops we finally made it to the property. Almost all the aunts and uncles were there and when they saw I brought Oreo, they couldn't believe it and howled. "A cat out camping; now that's a sight to see!"

Natalie and Gary were there with their new puppy Daisy. Daisy was a Jack Russel Terrier and as a puppy she loved her tennis ball. Everywhere Daisy went she had her ball in her mouth. Oreo wanted her ball. Gary tried to get it but Daisy wouldn't let go. He would grab it and she would just clench her teeth and jaw tighter, he literally picked Daisy up just by grabbing the ball in her mouth. She would dangle off it and still not let go. When she finally released her clench, Gary tossed it and Daisy took off like a dart. Oreo wanted to play too. He started running and pulled me right along with him. I was amazed how strong Oreo was. I'm sure it was quite the sight to watch a cat drag its owner.

Later that night we got ready for bed. Oreo and I were staying with mom and dad in their trailer. Mom and I shared a bed as Dad found the beds too small, he needed his own. I set up Oreo's food dishes and litter box and went to bed.

As I slept Oreo wandered around the tiny trailer. I slept peacefully, mom did not. When we awoke mom did not look very rested, in fact she looked downright angry. As we were eating breakfast outside with the family, mom explained her weariness. "Oreo wandered all night long! He'd eat his food, crunch crunch crunch then hop over my head to get to Caralee. Two minutes later he'd hop over my head again to go the litter box, scratch scratch scratch. Jump over my head again to get to Caralee! He did this all night long. Up, over, crunch, scratch! No, I didn't sleep at all!"

After we all finished laughing and cleaned up our breakfast dishes. Oreo and I headed home. As we drove home I chuckled at Oreo wearing out his welcome, his very first night.

We made it back to the property a few weeks later, but mom and dad didn't join us. Oreo and I spent a week at the property with Natalie and Daisy. Oreo loved sitting in the grass watching Natalie and I paint the tables. He loved going for walks down the lane with Daisy. Natalie and I enjoyed our chats while we all walked down the lane. Oreo took his time and Daisy urged him to hurry up.

Both Daisy and Oreo loved our movie nights. Natalie and I would make popcorn and Daisy would get her special treat, Oreo would get his kitty milk and we'd all pile into Natalie's trailer to watch a movie.

Oreo and Daisy became good friends. They were known as the most loved fur babies in the whole family, and they truly were.

Chapter 4

A New Bond

It was a typical Saturday afternoon, as I rushed around cleaning the apartment Oreo napped on the couch. When Oreo woke up it was time for me to have a break and play. Oreo loved to play fetch with his rubber ball. I'd throw it into the kitchen, Oreo would race across the carpet and the second he hit the linoleum, he'd slide on his butt using his claws as brakes while he caught the ball. He'd come back to me with the ball in his mouth and drop it at my feet. "Again mom, again," he'd say as I picked up the ball and threw it again.

After a few tosses, Oreo was tired. "That's odd" I thought. Oreo normally plays for about thirty minutes before he's ready for more cuddles. I followed him to the couch and sat down beside him and he crawled into my lap. Moments later he leapt off my lap and raced to his litter box. He scratched and scratched, jumped out and ran around the apartment while crying. He ran back to the box and scratched some more, scattering the litter everywhere. "What's wrong baby?" I asked. "Why are you mad at your box?" I grabbed the scooper to check the litter, but nothing except clean litter was in it. I could tell he was in pain so I rushed him to the vet.

He had bladder stones. Thankfully the vet thought they were small enough for him to pass, they were just starting to form and were crystalized. She gave me some pills to take home when she brought Oreo back to me. Oreo couldn't get out of her arms fast enough. He came running to me and I scooped him into my arms.

The rest of the day was filled with cuddles and purrs, head bunts and plenty of hugs and kisses. Oreo was quite content to sit on my lap while we waited for him to pass the painful stones.

Days later Oreo finally passed them. I knew he passed them before I saw the litter as he brought me his ball to play fetch. Oreo always found a way of telling me what he needed or wanted.

A couple months later and we were off to the vet again.

Our morning started as usual, Oreo was waking me gently by combing my hair and giving me a bath. I reached up and stroked his fur as I tried to get a few more minutes of sleep. Oreo didn't like extra snoozes so I'd get his paw tapped on my mouth. "Ok Oreo I'm getting up." I'd say.

He leapt off the bed and raced me to the kitchen. I filled myself a cup of water, changed his water, and topped up his food bowls. Then he raced me to the couch and jumped into my lap the second I sat down. Oreo loved his cuddle time in the mornings. Heaven forbid I slept in and had to race out the door. Oreo would not stand for skipping his special cuddle time. We cuddled for a bit before I got ready to go to work.

When we got out of the shower he went into the kitchen and ate a few kibbles. I had just finished getting dressed when I heard him cry. It was an awful, ear-piercing cry. I ran to the kitchen to find him covered in blood. His paw was in his mouth and blood was pouring out. My white and black kitten was now red and black. I couldn't possibly imagine what could cause what I was seeing. "Oreo what happened?" I cried, as I picked him up and raced out the door.

I frantically drove to the vet; thankfully the office was only three minutes away. I carried Oreo into the office, him in one arm and his food dish in the other. Oreo was instantly rushed to the back to be treated.

The vet came back after examining him and tells me he cut his tongue. I handed her the food dish and I showed her the piece that came out of his mouth. It looked like metal. "I just opened a new box of cat food this morning" I cried. She asked me to bring in the rest of the box so they could send it to the lab. (Weeks later I got the results… turns out that a piece of machinery at the processing plant broke and fell into the food.)

"Oreo is going to be ok" she assured me "He got it out without swallowing it, but cut his tongue. I'll give you a prescription to keep it from getting infected. Oreo is having a bit of a bath and as soon as he's cleaned up I will bring him to you."

Those few minutes felt like hours. Finally she came back with him wrapped in a towel. Oreo saw me and couldn't get out of her arms fast enough. He wanted mom. He wiggled and squirmed and came running. He ran to me as an injured or scared child runs to their mom. I scooped him up, buried my head in his fur and whispered, "I love you baby boy. Thank you Lord for protecting Oreo."

Not only did we go home with more medicine and a new bag of cat food, we left that office with an even greater bond. He was not just my cat. He was and forever will be, my precious baby boy.

Chapter 5

Christmas

Before I knew it our first Christmas arrived. Petland was promoting their Christmas pet program, pictures with Santa. Glenda and I decided it would be fun to have a picture of Oreo and Shylo with Santa.

I had to work that Saturday so Cory and Glenda picked up Oreo and took them to Petland. People were shocked to see a cat come in. Not just any cat, a cat on a leash. Oreo was an instant star. Even Santa was shocked as he said "Wow, what a special kitty you must be to walk on a leash." (He must have done alright on his leash even though he was still in training.)

Santa picked Shylo up in one arm and had Oreo placed in the other. Oreo was not impressed by being held by a stranger. He wanted down, but Santa was able to calm him long enough to get a picture. 15 years later this picture is still displayed proudly in my home.

By the time our second Christmas rolled around Oreo was fully trained. I made arrangements to bring him with me to our big family celebration in Alex, Alberta.

The days leading up to our trip, I continued scurrying around to finish my shopping and final preparations. Oreo was always so excited when I'd come home with presents to wrap. He loved "helping."

Just as I'd roll out the paper Oreo would lay on top of it. I would dangle a ribbon and he'd chase it as I cut the paper accordingly. When I started folding the paper around the gift he'd chase my fingers, and together we would place the tape. His claws would always puncture the paper and rumple up the neat folds. As I finished I chuckled at Oreo's wrapping skills. I contemplated redoing it while he napped, but didn't. "This year I had help", I thought as I continued placing ribbons and bows on the parcels.

Finally Christmas Eve arrived and Oreo and I drove to Morrison Meadows in Alex Alberta. It was a beautiful ranch, and had many cabins along with the main house. Oreo and I stayed in one of the cabins with Natalie, Gary, Daisy and my cousin Desiree.

Des and I shared a room, and as I sang to Oreo while we unpacked, she laughed hysterically at me. "Oh Caralee, I don't know anyone who could love a cat more than you" she said during a pause in her laughter.

Oreo wanted to investigate the cabin so I let him wander a bit, but it was almost supper time and I needed to go to the main house. I couldn't find him anywhere. "Where could he have gone?" I wondered. Before long everyone in the cabin was searching for him. I started panicking as I searched under the beds, in the closets, in the drawers, everywhere that could make a good, warm hiding place. Finally Natalie calls "I found him!" I rushed to Natalie's room and there he was snuggled into her clothes that she had placed into a drawer, moments before Oreo disappeared.

After a good laugh at my resourceful kitty finding a warm place to lie, I let out a huge sigh of relief. I brought Oreo back to my room and gave him one of my favorite hoodies to lie in. Once he was safely locked in the cabin I proceeded up to the main house.

The tree was beautifully decorated and overflowed with presents under it. Oreo of course had his own presents to open. Christmas morning came and Oreo wasn't too concerned with his new mice, balls or stringy toys. He wanted the paper, and there was plenty of it! Oreo jumped into the paper and watched it scatter. He rolled and scratched at it and jumped into the pile again. He also loved to chase me as I ran with the ribbons.

Later that afternoon, before Christmas dinner we had our family talent show. Oreo and Daisy were the stars of the show as they showed how special and well behaved they were. They both did their tricks of sit, beg and lay down. Daisy also rolled over and jumped through a hoop as she caught her ball. As everyone laughed at Oreo, he got stage fright and had a few near jumps off the stage, but with a bit of coaxing he also completed his tricks. Oreo was my pride and joy. The whole family, approx. fifty, grew to love him and accept him as my baby boy.

Oreo had so much fun that Christmas, he slept the whole way home. His nose was normally a pale pink, but when he dreamt it would turn bright pink. As I drove home I glanced at him sleeping beside me on the passenger seat. His nose was a bright pink and his paws had a slight twitch. I chuckled at the thought of him dreaming of scattering all the paper and chasing the ribbons.

"Oh Oreo, How you've won my heart" I whispered. "Thank you Lord for Oreo, thank you for giving me my precious baby boy."

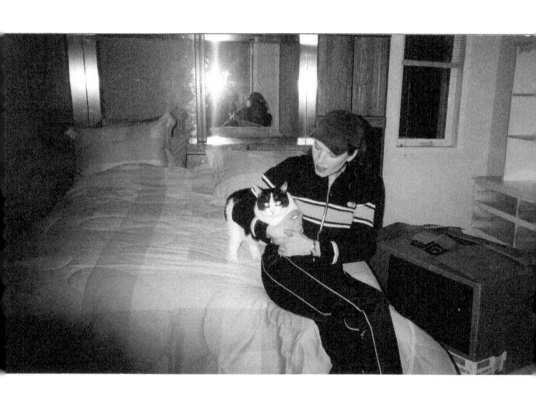

Chapter 6

A New Friend

In May of 2002 I bought our first home. Moving day quickly approached, and Oreo was anxiously waiting for me. I had him locked in the bedroom to keep him safe while the movers loaded up the apartment. I brought Oreo his kennel and he climbed in as I gathered his food and water bowls as well as his litter box. I took one last look at the empty apartment, locked up and loaded Oreo and his necessities into the car. Oreo was the last out of the apartment and the first into our new home.

Once the movers were gone I let Oreo out of the bedroom and let him roam his new home. He was proud as punch. He wandered through every room of the house and to show his approval he jumped up on to the breakfast bar, stretched out as far as he could then sprawled his eighteen pound body across the counter. Mom was miffed and hissed "Hey you silly Cat, I just cleaned that!" Oreo gave her a look that said "yeah and? This is my house. I'll lie here if I want to!"

Oreo seldomly jumped on the tables or counters, unless Mom was over. He knew she was not a fan of animals in the house, and had something to prove. Every time Mom came over Oreo would sprawl himself across the counter to remind her whose house it really was.

Oreo loved the space of the new home and the openness of it. It didn't take him long to find his favorite spots. He would lie on the beanbag chair I had in the office and be able to see every room in the house. He loved having his own sink in the ensuite. I'd brush my teeth at my sink while Oreo was playing with the water in his own. When I filled the jetted tub, he would jump on the ledge and play with the bubbles. Oreo and I were happy to have our own home, and I no longer needed to worry about being told I could not have a pet.

It wasn't long until Oreo knew all our neighbours. We would walk around the block and Oreo loved showing off how special he was. He held his head high and strutted proudly, as long as he was in control of where we were going. If I wanted to go a different direction, he would let me know by lying down. Hence his nickname "Mop" still applied.

"Mop" loved his walks and the security of his leash. Whenever a dog approached he'd lie down and wait for me to pick him up. Oreo knew he was my world and I wouldn't let anything bad happen to him.

Shortly after we moved in Rickie, my cousin just got a new puppy. Since Oreo got along so well with Shylo and Daisy I thought he'd enjoy another friend. Mom and dad were already on their way so I told Rickie to come over too.

When the doorbell rang Oreo took off like a dart to welcome our guests. Oreo was staring out the glass paned door, and was slightly growling. Rickie, Asher, and my parents arrived at the same time. I picked Oreo up as I opened the door, but he wasn't having it. He was saying loud and clear with his hissing and growling "This is my house! Get that dog out of here!"

As Asher, the husky pup, continued following behind Rickie, Oreo flew out of my arms as he hissed and growled. Then out came the claws and fur started flying. Asher whimpered and cowered behind Rickie. I couldn't believe Asher didn't even bark or try to bite, just cowered and whimpered.

I finally caught Oreo and calmed him down, while Rickie escorted Asher out to the back yard. "Oreo," I scolded "That's not a nice way to welcome our guests." I kissed his head as I continued "I'm sorry honey I thought you'd like a new friend." Oreo quickly calmed and I went outside to meet the puppy.

Asher was a beautiful black, grey and white Husky and very high spirited. How such a high spirited dog could get his butt kicked by a cat remains a mystery.

The adults continued our visit as Oreo and Asher stared at each other through the window. Every time Oreo growled or hissed, Asher whimpered. Neither Oreo nor Asher got hurt, so we could see the humor in their encounter and enjoy our visit. Dad on the other hand, was in the process of closing the door when Oreo flew at Asher, his leg had a few claw marks, but nothing a bandage and a few cuddles from Oreo couldn't cure.

Oreo liked everyone and won everyone's hearts. Everyone that is, except Asher.

Chapter 7

Cat's eye view

Oreo loved it when I would come home with loads of groceries; he liked to play in the bags that I scrunched into a ball and tossed into a pile. He loved the sound of the crinkle as he'd jump into them and scatter them all around. He continued playing in the bags while I put away my groceries. I was only about half way through when all of a sudden he took off like a dart. A bag was chasing him. I ran after him, up the stairs down the hall and into the spare bedroom. Somehow he managed to roll into the bags and get a handle around his neck.

"Oreo baby, you're ok, come out from under the bed." I assured him. "Let mommy help you." I continued to beg as he crawled under the bed and crouched down by the back wall. I couldn't reach him and I couldn't coax him out. I frantically started tearing the bed apart, flinging the pillows and the blankets, and heaving the mattresses off the bed. Finally I reached Oreo, and was able to get the bag off his neck. "Well I guess that's the end of that game." I said as I kissed his head, "Your only four and have already used six lives."

Oreo was famous for getting into mischief and compromising situations.

Another evening I was cleaning everything I could, light fixtures, switch plates, baseboards etc. I even removed the heat and cooling vents to wash them up. Once they were washed and dried I went around putting them back on and noticed once again Oreo wasn't at my heel. I was searching and calling for him, and then I heard it. "Oh no," I cried "Oreo get out of the vents, come to mommy!", but he was having too much fun in the tin tunnels he found.

I ran to the basement and pounded on the vents to try to scare him away from the furnace, but he just found a different tunnel to crawl through. I ran upstairs to turn off the thermostat and the fan to make sure he didn't get a blast of heat coming, then ran downstairs again to continue trying to coax him out of the vents.

After a few minutes, I was getting quite worried and started wondering who to call for help. "The fire department?" I wondered. I decided to call my dad he always knew what to do, or so I thought. I ran upstairs to call dad, as I was racing back to the basement mom answered and without so much of a hello I blurt out "Oreo is in the vents! Who do I call to get him out?" After a few seconds of silence mom asks "What vents? How in the world would he get into a vent?" I explained "I was cleaning and took off the registers and he crawled through one." Mom instantly cracked up, laughing hysterically. She pulled herself together long enough to explain my plight to dad, now both of them were laughing. "Seriously this isn't funny how do I get him out? I don't want him to get cooked by the furnace." I retorted. That only made them laugh harder. After dad made a comment about fried kitty being for supper I realized they weren't going to be much help and I had to find a way to coax Oreo out myself.

I'm sure my neighbours were wondering what in the world was going on at my house with all the racket coming from my basement. I was still banging on the vents an hour later when Oreo finally appeared and started to claw his way up my leg. His ears were slightly tilted backwards and he looked quite annoyed with me, I could just picture him saying "Seriously mom, could you be any more annoying? I was having fun!"

I was so relieved to finally have him back in my arms safe and sound; I barely noticed the dirty paw prints he left all over my white carpet. "Oh Oreo, my curious boy, mommy needs to learn to see things from a cat's eye view."

Chapter 8

Ferocious Feline

Cory, Glenda and Shylo came over one Sunday afternoon. Oreo was tired after our walk and was sleeping on the couch. I was playing with Shylo and her tug rope toy. Shylo was a well-tempered shiatzu and loved to play. She would get quite excited with her toys and loved to try to tug it out of your hands.

I was about five feet away from the couch Oreo was napping on, while I played tug of war with Shylo. She barked and growled as dogs do when playing. Oreo was not happy that Shylo barked or growled at his mom. He instantly woke up and leapt off the couch, over the coffee table, jumped over me and tackled Shylo.

Poor Shylo didn't know what happened. After a few rolls with Oreo, Shylo stood up and shook her head with a stunned look on her face as if to say "What was that for?" Oreo stood his ground, and gave her a look back that said "Nobody growls at my mom!" After a few minutes of laughter from the adults Oreo and Shylo made up. Oreo curled into my lap and Shylo wandered over to Glenda.

Not even I could have imagined my sweet cuddly kitten could turn into a ferocious guard kitty. I knew than that Oreo loved me as much as I loved him, and he was bound and bent to protect his mom. It was truly remarkable to see his love made so abundantly clear to all.

Chapter 9

Welcome Home

When my second niece, Teagan, was born I went to Ft. McMurray to help out with the kids. I was excited to see all of them, but the thought of leaving Oreo behind broke my heart. My Uncle Rob had just moved to Calgary and didn't have a place to live yet. He was more than willing to stay at my house and look after Oreo while I was away.

I started packing while Oreo watched me fold my clothes and place them in the suitcase. He jumped into the suitcase and played with the clothes I placed in. Once I had everything refolded I zipped up the suitcase and brought it downstairs and placed it at the front door. Oreo sensed something was different. He moped around the house until he found his leash. He picked it up in his teeth dragged it to the door, plopped it on top of the suitcase, jumped up and laid down as if to say "I'm coming too mom!"

He wasn't too happy with me when I put the leash away upon Uncle Rob's arrival and proceeded to leave without him.

I missed Oreo terribly, but had an excellent three weeks with my nieces. Kyla was so excited to have auntie there she would wake me up at 5:30 every morning, and kept me busy all day every day, by the end of the three weeks I was exhausted. By the time I left I was filled with a new respect for stay home moms.

My plane finally landed in Calgary and I couldn't wait to get home to Oreo. Three weeks was too long to be away from my boy. The second I walked in Oreo saw me and came running. I had only a few minutes of cuddles and purrs until he jumped out of my lap and turned away from me. He stuck his nose up in the air as he walked away and his body language spoke loud and clear "How dare you leave me!"

I dragged my suitcase upstairs, expecting Oreo to follow, but he didn't. Once I finished unpacking I headed downstairs, grabbed a pop out of the fridge and just went to take a sip when Oreo jumped onto the island and leaped towards me.

The opened can of coke crashed to the floor as I tried to catch my flying cat. "I guess this means you forgive me?" I chuckled, as Oreo rolled in my arms to have both hands pet him. Oreo and I cuddled together for a couple hours before he'd let me clean up the mess he created.

When I met up with my aunts and Uncle Rob that Saturday afternoon, they shared stories of Rob and Oreo. Rob loved having Oreo nestle into his lap, and Oreo wasn't shy at teaching Rob exactly how he liked to be petted. I could just picture Oreo saying "Both hands please not just one, pet and rub at the same time, scratch my ears and my chin then repeat. Whatever you do don't forget the belly rubs."

I found it quite humorous as they shared stories of Rob and Oreo and how Uncle Rob would constantly be covered in cat hair. "If I wore white I was covered in black hair, when I wore black I was covered in white! I couldn't win!" He chuckled as he continued "But he most certainly is a special cat."

I was one proud momma as Rob shared how Oreo won his heart.

Chapter 10

Home is Where the Heart is

In March of 2003 I decided to get my real estate license and become a realtor. Oreo loved having me home. He would sit on my lap as I searched the listings on the computer and loved to chase the pen as I made my notes. When it was time for a break Oreo wasn't shy about letting me know. He would hop off my lap and onto the keyboard, and then lay down on top of it, saying loud and clear, "That's enough work mom, its play time!"

Every day around 11:45am Oreo was ready for playtime. We would play fetch and he would chase me around the house with his stringy toy. He loved to sneak up on it and have to jump for it. After about thirty minutes of play Oreo was ready for a nap and I could get some more work done.

Working from home enabled me to learn Oreo's routine. Mornings were his prime cuddle moments. And he had plenty of energy to play before he ate lunch and have his afternoon nap. As much as possible I scheduled my appointments around his nap times. To this day, I don't like having to leave the house before noon as Oreo wouldn't be ready for his nap until 12:30pm. Oreo was the center of my world and my top priority.

In 2005 I decided to sell the house and downsize. As I was out showing my client prospective homes another realtor was showing mine. Before I left I brought Oreo and his necessities downstairs and locked him in the basement to keep him safe during the showing.

I pulled up to my driveway and imagine my surprise when I saw Oreo on my front lawn coming to greet me. He looked mighty proud of himself as if to say "Look Mom, no leash!" I was relieved that I got home when I did and scooped him into my arms as I sighed "Well that was perfect timing. What would mommy do if you got lost or hit by a car?" I planted kisses on his head all the way up the porch and into the house.

Once I saw the lock on the basement had been picked my relief quickly turned to anger as I thought, "How dare he pick the lock against my instructions!" My temper was boiling as I dialed the realtor's number. When the realtor answered I reminded him of our conversation when I agreed to a showing, one rule "Do not let the cat out!" I also reminded him "Not only did I mention it to every realtor who showed my home, but it was also on the mandatory instruction sheet with the listing, in all capital letters, bold print, underlined and exclamation points. Not to mention the basement door was locked with a sign on the door stating the basement is undeveloped which may be shown when owner is present." To which he replied "Sorry no English" and hung up.

"My house is no longer for sale" I grumbled as I went to the computer and immediately cancelled my listing. Once my listing was cancelled I prayed that God would bring a buyer to me, since I couldn't trust my fellow realtors to follow my instructions concerning Oreo's safety and well- being.

God answered my request and the house sold Dec 2005.

Moving day approached a little too quickly. Both Oreo and I loved that house and had many special memories in it. As we took one last tour of our empty house, I kissed his head and spoke softly in his ear, "Home is where the heart is baby boy. You are my heart. We will make more memories in our new home."

With that Oreo crawled into his kennel and we proceeded to our new home.

Chapter 11
Everything is a Game

Oreo missed the openness of the old house, the breakfast bar and his own special sink. It took him a while to settle in, but eventually he found his new favorite spots. Oreo loved the stairway being straight up and down, he loved to have races. He would give me about a three second start before he would come charging from behind me and pass me. When he got to the top, he'd peek around the corner with a grin that said "I beat you mom!" When we went down the stairs he'd run and hide around the island, just waiting to sneak up and pounce at me when I made it to the kitchen.

We discovered that this house was perfect for playing hide and seek. Oreo loved to hide and jump out at me, and get me to chase him (like I would pretend to chase a toddler). He loved to hide behind the island and peek around the corner as I went to hide around the other wall. He would pounce around the corner and run in circles as I went to hide again. Hide and seek became our nightly ritual before we would race up the stairs to go to bed. He loved hide and seek so much that he would not let me go upstairs without at least three turns each.

Oreo had a natural talent to turn even the most mundane tasks into a game. He loved laundry day. I would just get a basket of clothes sorted and without fail; Oreo would jump into the basket dig himself a nice cozy bed and have a nap. I would be forced to gather the second load since he had claimed the first.

In his later years he preferred to jump on my back and nestle into my neck while he watched me toss the clothes into the appropriate basket. He always had to be close to me and if my arms or hands were full my back or neck would do. I learned to do many things while I was hunched over with him snuggling my neck, including my makeup.

One of his favorite things about laundry day was "helping" me make beds. He would jump onto the mattress just as I was fluffing the sheet and wait for it to fall on him. When I started to straighten it he would grab the sheet away from me and roll into it. He loved getting tangled up in the nice clean warm sheets. "Oh what fun!" he'd say, as he chased my fingers while I untangled him from the sheet. He loved to scurry under the sheets chasing my fingers as I tucked in each corner. He repeated this game with all the sheets and blankets for all three beds. With Oreo's help it took over an hour just to make beds. I guess time management wasn't too high on his list and I wouldn't have had it any other way.

Chapter 12

A Sister for Oreo

In May of 2006, I received a call regarding a cat that had been abandoned in an apartment. The owners were out of town for an extensive period and the people who were supposed to look after it weren't. The poor cat had no food, no water, and the litter box was overflowing so there were many accidents on the carpet.

Once I got off the phone, I quickly gathered some of Oreo's supplies to help the kitty and assess the situation. I raced downtown and as I walked into the apartment I was horrified to see the condition the poor cat was in and the environment it was living in.

The cat's name was Alley and was nothing but skin and bone. Every bone was sticking out of her body. Her medium long fur was badly matted and felt like petting a wire brush. She was very skittish and hid, while my cousin and I tried to clean up some of the mess. The food dishes were left right beside her litter box so there was dirty litter in the dishes. A whole can of moist food was left out for her, but was dried up and covered in flies and litter. My heart was breaking for this poor kitty.

Once we had the mess cleaned up I was able to coax Alley to come to me and give her some attention. She sat on my lap and let me pet her head, if I tried to pet her farther than half way down her back she would hiss. As I sat with Alley, I thought of Oreo and wondered if he would accept another cat into our home. I was also concerned at the possibility of Alley having a contagious disease that could be passed to Oreo, so I knew I had to leave Alley at the apartment for now.

A few days went by with me checking in on Alley daily and gaining her trust. I sat with her for about an hour and half each evening petting and brushing her, while trying to nurture her back to health. She was so skinny and you could see every bone sticking out, touching her was not a very pleasurable experience. I was so angry that anyone could starve an animal and leave it to die. I knew she needed more care than ninety minutes a day so I decided to bring her to the vet and have her tested for anything that could be passed to Oreo.

My heart sank as he explained that her test came back as positive for feline FIV (aids). I knew I couldn't put Oreo in jeopardy to try to save her, but since there were cases of false positives I asked to repeat the test to be certain. Thankfully the second tests came back negative and I was given the all clear to take her home. I had company coming in a few days and I knew that was not a good time to introduce Alley to a new home, so I once again enlisted the help of my aunt Natalie. She agreed to have Alley come to her house for the week until my company left.

At the end of the week I picked Alley up and brought her home. Alley didn't have any disease that could be passed to Oreo, but she was still sick so I kept the cats separate. Alley had her necessities in the basement and Oreo's litter was brought upstairs to the spare bathroom.

As I expected Oreo let me know when it was time to introduce them. One evening I was getting dinner ready and heard the cats playing through the door, Oreo happily agreed to have his leash on while I let Alley roam her new home.

I was amazed at how quickly Oreo accepted her. Alley roamed the house and marched upstairs, saw my bed and made herself comfortable. Oreo laid down just outside the bedroom door and they stared at each other for a few minutes while Oreo blinked at her and held her gaze with his half open eyes. His eyes were telling her "Welcome to our home. You will be happy here."

They took to each other pretty quickly and I was amazed at how quickly Alley returned to health. It took her only about six weeks to gain three pounds, and between my brushing and her grooming, her fur was starting to get softer.

Oreo was so patient and loving towards her he accepted her without hesitation. She had rule over everything. Everything that is except mommy.

Oreo and Alley worked out their new routine and how mommy time would work. Oreo had mommy time until Alley would make her way downstairs from the bedroom and loudly meow, pronouncing it's her turn. Alley would sit with me for about half an hour until she would once again loudly pronounce its bedtime.

The three of us would make our way upstairs and Oreo and Alley would play as I got ready for bed. Then Alley would hop on the bed and guard it from Oreo. They were both possessive of their mommy time. She would stare Oreo down while he stayed on the floor until she had enough cuddles and made her way to her side of the bed. Oreo then would jump up and nestle under the covers for more cuddles. Oreo loved to cuddle, in all our wonderful years together he was never more than an arm's length away.

Oreo was so special and good for the soul. He was Alley's greatest nurturer. She had been through so much and was scared of everyone and everything. Oreo taught her to trust again. He taught her to love and to accept love in return. He taught her to play and he brought her back to life.

Chapter 13

Unfailing Love

Cory, Glenda and my nieces came for a visit and spent the weekend with Oreo and I, while Natalie cared for Alley. Kyla was three and Teagan was one. They laughed and giggled as Oreo would pounce and jump for his mouse on a string. I would swing it high and low, back and forth and Oreo would hide then sneak and pounce on it.

Kyla wanted to try so I gave her the string and Oreo happily continued pouncing and jumping and putting on a show for the girls. Kyla tried to swing it as wildly as auntie, Oreo jumped for it and caught the string, but Kyla's finger was too far down the string and he caught her finger in the process with his claw.

Tears started to flow and Kyla raised her hand to spank Oreo. I had Oreo out of her reach before she could touch him and hugged Kyla close while I spoke to her soothingly "Oreo would never hurt you on purpose. He was so excited to play with you. He's just used to my fingers being higher up. It was an accident and we never, ever hit animals."

Once I bandaged her finger she wanted to play with Oreo again, so I found another string from an old hoodie and tied it to his toy.

She enjoyed the extra-long string and all weekend long she played with Oreo.

She fell in love with Oreo that weekend and told her mom she wanted a cat too. A few years later her wish came true and they rescued a 9yr old cat, Gretchen, from the humane society.

That same weekend Teagan was only one and still learning to walk. We were all upstairs in the loft playing with the girls. Oreo of course was up there too, he always had to be in the middle of the action. He was laying in the middle of the floor when Teagan got up to walk. "Oh no" I gasped, as she fell right on top of Oreo. "Good he's ok" I sighed as he scrambled to get out from under her.

Once he was free he looked up at her as if to say "Hey I was lying there, what did I do to deserve that?" I was nervous that he may scratch or bite her, but that thought never crossed his mind. He was so gentle and loving and must have known it was just an accident.

When Teagan got up to walk again he cautiously followed behind her, ready to get out of her way when she fell. When she did fall Oreo was always there to offer his love and would rub up against her to encourage her to try again.

Oreo was one incredibly special and unique cat. He was my comfort and joy, my biggest fan and a true example of unfailing love.

Chapter 14

Eye on the Sky

Shortly after Alley joined our family I had some friends in for a game night. Oreo loved company, Alley hated it. Alley was a one person cat and was scared of everyone and everything. She had two favorite hiding spots and the second the doorbell rang she would take off to the basement to hide. Oreo would always race me to the door as he expected to be the first one greeted. Every time the doorbell rang I'd have cats racing in different directions, it was quite the ordeal to time the opening of the door just right.

Oreo enjoyed all the attention he received and if anyone didn't like cats, he would make it his mission to win them over and he always did.

One of my guests asked to see Alley, so I went to find her and brought her out of hiding. I placed Alley into her arms, but Alley wasn't happy, neither was Oreo. Alley wiggled and squirmed her way out of the young woman's arms and took off running. Oreo started to chase Alley, and I chased Oreo.

I knew I was about to have a cat fight. Oreo was miffed that someone didn't pet him before Alley. That's the rule. "Oops, my fault" I thought, "I shouldn't have brought Alley up without making sure she petted Oreo first."

As Oreo hissed and spit at Alley, I clapped my hands and firmly said "No!" Oreo sulked on his way back to the company, but eventually settled into my lap. I learnt a valuable lesson to ensure everyone gives Oreo a little attention before Alley, as it was the cats' rule.

The next weekend was a beautiful Saturday afternoon, the windows were open and the birds were chirping. Oreo decided it was too nice to be cooped up in the house. I was washing windows when Oreo tapped my leg with his paw with his leash in his mouth. "You want to go for a walk? Ok let me finish this window then we will go," I said.

Anything Oreo asked for he got, I guess he knew his wish was my command. I put away the cleaning supplies and quickly checked on Alley. When I came back downstairs Oreo was waiting at the back door with his leash.

Oreo was a sturdy cat; with all the exercise he received his muscles were very strong. However I probably fed him a few too many treats during training as he weighed almost eighteen pounds. His tummy was only a couple inches from the floor and when he ran it jiggled back and forth. He outgrew his cat harness the first year and now needed a dog's harness.

Oreo loved his walks so much that he stepped into the harness himself as I adjusted the shoulder and neck straps. "Ok Oreo you're all done" I said as I began to open the door. "Oreo wait! I have to close the door!" I exclaimed as he was running of the deck. My one arm was stretched with him tugging me his way while I stretched the other arm to close the door.

He was anxious to get outside and tour the complex. We walked around the entire complex and Oreo still wasn't ready to go inside. I let him lay in the grass while I watched him play from the deck and Alley watched from the window.

While Oreo played with the grass I heard a bird squawking. I looked up and saw a big black crow swooping towards Oreo. I leapt off the deck in a panic, as I threw my body over Oreo. The crow was angry and as I ran towards the house with Oreo shielded by my body, the crow continued squawking and swooping towards us.

Finally we made it into the house, and Alley was running in circles meowing loudly. Once she saw Oreo was safe they both took off running upstairs to the office window to watch the crow circle around the yard. Both cats started chirping back at the crow as if to say "Watch it bird, you picked on the wrong kitty!"

Finally the crow went back to its perch on my neighbour's roof and the cats settled down.

Oreo continued to enjoy his escapes outside, but we always stayed close to home while I kept my eye on the sky.

Chapter 15

Life Altered

June of 2009, our morning started as usual, Alley was sleeping in and Oreo was anxiously waiting for me to wake up. Once I made my coffee Oreo and I raced downstairs to cuddle as I organized my day.

Oreo once again leapt off my lap and raced to the litter box. Scratching and scattering the litter all over. He jumped out of the box and back into it, crying constantly and was unable to urinate again.

"Oreo do you need to go to the vet?" I asked him as I brought his kennel out. Oreo blinked his eyes for yes and crawled into the opened kennel. We raced to the vet's office and they determined he once again had bladder stones. Unfortunately this time they were too large for him to pass, he needed surgery.

As the vet told me the diagnosis I fell apart and tears started to flow, buckets of tears. I couldn't afford surgery and didn't have pet health insurance. I left the vets office with Oreo and a heavy heart, fearing I wouldn't have time to come up with the money.

I called my parents to ask them to pray for Oreo and I, as I explained my money situation. After considering the alternatives they offered to pay for the surgery. I was so relieved to have an option, yet extremely humbled as I have always prided myself on being independent and working hard to provide for myself. Despite my wounded pride, I was so thankful that they were helping me save Oreo.

Loosing Oreo was not an option, it would literally kill me. He was my comfort and my joy, he was my everything. I made up my mind right then and there, to quit my real estate career and go to work full time for my parents to earn a steady pay cheque. As soon as I got off the phone with my mom, I made the appointment for surgery the following morning.

Oreo and I showed up at 8:00am, as I signed all the waivers I had to face the reality that surgery comes with great risks as well. I was on pins and needles all day as I waited to hear how my boy was doing.

Finally the call came. "Oreo made it through surgery! He's going to be ok!" I exclaimed as I ran out of my office and raced across town to pick him up.

Oreo was very groggy, but happy to see me. We went home with four medications to control his pain and keep infection away. Thankfully Oreo was very easy to pill.

About a week into recovery I gave him his medicine as usual. This time he refused to have the fourth pill, it was tramadol, a time release capsule the size of a horse pill. I had opened his mouth and got it to the back of his tongue, but this time he tried to spit it out. He bit into it and instantly started foaming at the mouth excessively.

It was horrifying to see my baby with that much white foam coming out! I instantly panicked and brought him into emergency. They tried to assure me that he will be ok since he got the pill out without swallowing it, so I brought him home.

A couple days later, I woke up in a start sensing something was wrong with Oreo. I rolled over and noticed he wasn't on the bed, he was on the floor. I leapt out of bed crying "No, God No!" Oreo was having a seizure.

I had never been so scared in my life. I've heard of people having seizures, but have never witnessed one. I didn't know what to do. I knelt down beside him and stroked his fur as his little body crunched up and his eyes rolled into his head. "Mommy loves you." I cried, "Come back to me baby boy!"

It seemed like hours, but it lasted only a few short minutes. Oreo came through and didn't know what happened. He curled up into my lap as I buried my head into his fur and cried. Once Oreo crawled out of my lap, I hopped into the shower to get ready to take him to the vet.

He stayed at the hospital all day while I was at work. When I went to pick him up I was thankful he didn't have another seizure, but they also were unable to give me any answers as to what caused the seizure.

My gut told me it is one of three things, a complication of surgery, biting the tramadol or a reaction to all the medicine combined. I longed for answers, I spent hours each day researching everything I could, but no answer came.

Oreo started having seizures daily and got up to about five a day. I was taking him to the vet daily and leaving him at the hospital while I went to work. He would not have a seizure at the hospital; he always waited until I was with him.

The worst seizure was on his way downstairs to go to the litter-box. He had one on the stairs. I caught him as he started to fall and he seized in my lap. I cried and cried and pleaded with God to heal my boy. I also asked for strength to let him go, if he won't be healed.

He was having up to five seizures daily for a month straight, then after the stair incident they instantly stopped. I guess God chose to heal him. Thank you Lord for saving my boy!

I was always on pins and needles for the next few years, praying he wouldn't have another one. They were absolutely horrifying!

Oreo developed arthritis shortly after, probably due to the pressure on his legs during those seizures I assumed. He started slowing down a little bit and not playing as hard or as long. He still loved to jump, but I could tell he was in a bit of pain when he did. This is what started our elevator game, which I'll save for another chapter.

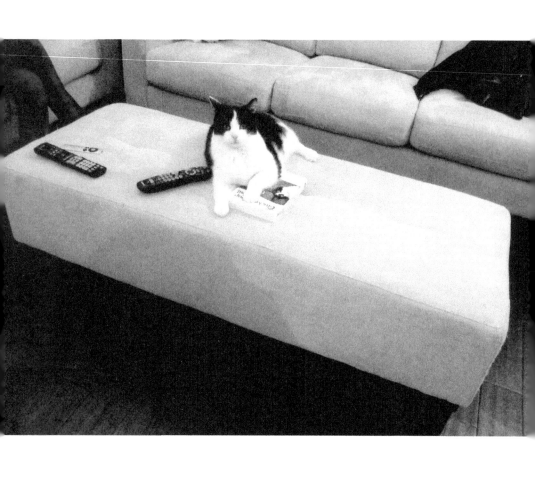

Chapter 16

Just Purr

It was a typical Sunday afternoon; Oreo was napping on the bean bag chair in the office while I scurried around to finish cleaning. I was putting the vacuum away when Oreo ran out of the office in a panic and ran downstairs. "What's wrong baby?" I asked as I followed behind him. Once I reached the bottom of the stairs I saw something white. "A claw?" I wondered. As I was trying to figure out what I was looking at, Oreo had a seizure, the first one in a year and a half. Before I had time to get his emergency diazepam, the seizure was over.

I quickly put the claw in a sandwich bag and rushed Oreo to emergency. The vet examined Oreo and it seemed the seizure was triggered by pain. It wasn't a claw after all, it was a tooth. He somehow managed to lose his fang tooth.

I was once again a nervous wreck; Oreo seemed to be seizure free for the last year and a half. I made an appointment with our regular vet the next day. Dr. Tasha Kean was so patient with me and Oreo absolutely adored her. Words can't begin to describe my gratefulness for Dr. Kean.

Oreo had developed a fear of pills since he bit the tramadol and was no longer easy to pill; in fact he was impossible to pill. Dr. Kean was determined to find a way to help Oreo take his medicine. We tried pill pockets which worked for a few weeks until he discovered he could eat around the pill. We tried flavored chewable tablets, but he was too smart for those as well. We tried mixing it in his food and in his favorite snacks, but before we could find the right medicine for Oreo, he had another horrific episode.

I was getting ready for church when Oreo came running into the bathroom. His head was shaking, legs were bouncing back and forth, tail twitching side to side and his fur was rippling, all the while he was biting himself uncontrollably as he ran.

I was in shock as I have never seen anything like it and didn't know what it was. I rushed him to emergency and he was diagnosed with rolling skin disease.

"Rolling what?" I asked. She explained "His body is so sensitive that even air touching his fur can cause him severe pain. The twitching and biting is a different type of seizure."

After many tears and asking my numerous questions I took Oreo home. Through my tears I assured him "We'll figure this out baby. Remember our song from Oliver and Company 'You and me together will be. Forever you'll see, you and me together will be.' I'm not giving up so don't you."

We had many adjustments to make as Oreo became sensitive to everything. He could no longer have his fish oil or his favorite treats as he was sensitive to seafood. I couldn't change the brand of his litter or even my laundry detergent. The slightest change could trigger a sensitivity seizure.

Finally Dr. Kean had the answer, she spoke to the lab and they could make the gabapentin medicine in a transdermal gel that gets applied in his ear. Oreo loved having his ears massaged as I rubbed the medicine in his ear. Within a month the seizures were controlled and Oreo learnt that the medicine made him feel better. Before I'd even look at the clock Oreo would lay down in front of the pantry door telling me "Medicine time mom!" He was more reliable than any alarm clock.

Throughout all these episodes Oreo's sweet, loving personality never changed. Our play time was a little shorter and we could no longer enjoy our walks outside so we increased our cuddle time. Oreo loved to be cradled like a baby and stare into my eyes as I rocked him. As we sat on the couch he would wrap his legs around my arm and curl into my chest as he hugged me.

I received a Chicken soup book for Christmas that year entitled "I can't believe my cat did that!" Every night I would read Oreo a story from that book about a special kitty. Oreo loved story time! The second he saw me pick up the book he would jump into my lap and stick his head into the book as I read. If I didn't know better I would have sworn he was reading along with me.

His favorite story was about a cat named Appleton. Appleton lost his tail and when he was found he was sitting on a bench purring. Reading that story reminded me that cats don't just purr to show contentment, they also purr to calm themselves in stressful situations.

Oreo and I adopted Appleton's lesson to "Just Purr" and it became our new slogan. As the years went by I learnt to recognize the early signs of any possible sensitivity/pain type seizure. As Oreo would run to me, I would kneel down and rub his head and brush his back while reminding him to "Just Purr."

Oreo loved his book and whenever he felt it was story time he would jump up on the ottoman and place his paws on the book telling me "Story time mom." When we finished reading all the stories in his book I promised him I'd write him his own book. "A book all about you," I promised as I kissed his head.

Before I started his book I wrote him short stories about all my previous pets. I read him stories of my dogs, Mark and Lady and my cats, Ginger, Smokey, Tiger, Misty, Leopard and Patches. Oreo loved hearing stories of his brothers and sisters, but his favorite was still Appleton and his reminder to "Just Purr."

Chapter 17

Keeping Watch

Finally by January 2012 I had Alley completely retrained to use her litter box. Alley had been so traumatized by being left alone and the conditions she was living in, it took time to completely earn her trust and correct the psychological issues she had.

The carpet in the basement was horrid and had to go and the carpet upstairs was scratched to threads, as Alley didn't have any toys or scratching posts at her previous home. I had a scratching post in every room of the house, but 90% of them were made of carpet. I learned a valuable lesson from Alley that cats learn by texture of what is deemed acceptable to scratch.

I decided it was time to rip out the nasty carpet and replace with new flooring. Neither Oreo nor Alley liked the hardwood or the laminate. They had to relearn how to walk down the stairs, but within a few days they were racing up and down sounding more like horses than cats.

I got used to Oreo's thump, thump, thump down the stairs as he would race me down. I always knew where each cat was just by the sound of their paws tapping on the floor. Alley's was quiet and gentle unless she was trying to get Oreo to play or letting me know its past my bedtime.

She would run up and down the stairs and through every room in the house meowing loudly saying, "Bedtime mom!" Oreo would leap off my lap and run upstairs within a few minutes of her carrying on. They would play as I got ready for bed and Alley would hop up, cuddle me then proceed to her side of the bed. Oreo would then hop up on his side and snuggle in. I now had a cat sleeping on each side of my head, with each of their paws pinning my hair to the pillow. It was very peaceful and soothing to fall asleep to the rhythm of their purrs.

Our lives were once again adjusted as my brother got divorced and his kids moved to Calgary. When Cory's time off would allow, about once a month, he would stay at my house with the kids for a week. As the girls were still young, it took some adjustment for all of us to find a rhythm.

I had only one rule. The safety of Oreo and Alley come first in my home. Of course I love my nieces and their well-being is also top priority, but that is their dad's responsibility, the cats are mine.

I had numerous conversations with the girls of what cat safety entails. "We never let the cats outside, and we don't leave plastic bags lying around or small toys. We throw garbage in the garbage and we always put the icky toilet seat down, so the cats can't drink from dirty water." Not too much to ask I thought. Throughout the years I would constantly be picking up something that could be potentially dangerous, but Oreo and I loved having Cory and the kids stay with us.

Oreo always loved company and he especially loved the commotion and laughter of the girls. He was constantly getting into the playroom to watch them play and wanted to join in on their fun.

At bedtime I would read the girls a story before I tucked them in. One night they decided they wanted me to read a cat story from Oreo's book. I went downstairs and grabbed the book off the ottoman, Oreo of course saw me take his book and came rushing after me.

As I sat on the edge of the bed with the girls and started to read about Appleton, the cat that lost his tail, Oreo hopped into my lap and also enjoyed the story. The girls laughed at Oreo and how he said "Hey that's my book! You can't read that without me!"

As I tucked the girls in and kissed them goodnight Oreo also rubbed up against each girl in unison as if he was also saying goodnight.

One evening after the girls were in bed, Cory and I decided to watch a movie. I was lying on the couch with Oreo on my chest. As I stroked his fur he'd purr and every few minutes he'd lift his head begging for kisses. I'd kiss his head and he would nestle back in.

Cory was not a cat person, but even he couldn't deny how special Oreo was. As Oreo and I continued our usual snuggles and kisses, Cory out of nowhere pronounced "Holy does that cat ever love you!"

I of course replied with "We love each other. Oreo is my world. I dread the day when he is no longer with me, losing him will probably kill me too." Cory said he worries about that day too, knowing our bond and that Oreo has been my lifeline for the past twelve years.

When it was time for me to go to bed I couldn't sleep. Alley hated having company so she was in her hiding place, and Oreo felt he had more people to watch over and protect. When Cory and the girls were here, Oreo slept in the loft so he could watch over every room.

I could no longer sleep without the rhythm of both cat's purrs. Eventually when the house was quiet for long enough Alley would make her way upstairs to her pillow. Oreo also decided mom was his top priority so he also eventually nestled in beside me. He knew I needed his purr to put me to sleep. He would hop up and lick my hair and go to sleep, purring all night long.

Chapter 18

Oreo the Mascot

Oreo in all his years never fussed when it was time for a vet visit. In fact he was trained to let me know if he needed one. I would ask him if he needed to go to the vet and he would close his eyes for yes and open wide for no. To confirm I would get his kennel and he would either go in or not.

In Dec 2012 at Oreo's annual wellness exam he was diagnosed with hyperthyroidism. Since Dr. Kean has been his regular vet since 2009 she knew his history and didn't waste any time in getting his medicine specially made for him in a transdermal gel pen.

Oreo liked Dr. Tasha and she always had treats for him. After Oreo had a few too many self feeds, I decided he needed to work for them. Oreo had no problem showing Dr. Kean how special he was as he sat, lied down and begged.

Dr. Kean was shocked as he put on his show and asked me to get a video of it so she could submit it for consideration on their website. "Oreo could be our mascot." She said.

Oreo did not like the camera. After many attempts I finally captured him on video, but he was camera shy and refused to lie down. I guess he wasn't as excited as I was for him to be a mascot.

A few months later Oreo decided he wanted to nap in my bedframe shelving. He had developed arthritis a few years prior so we developed the elevator game. He would jump onto the bed then onto my back to get into the appropriate shelf. When he awoke from his naps he'd quietly meow letting me know he was ready to come out. I'd offer him my back and he'd jump to the bed to the floor.

Even though he had arthritis Oreo loved to jump. Jumping up didn't seem to be an issue, getting down was. When he jumped on the counter, even though he wasn't supposed to, I'd offer him my back and he would walk on. Once he was stable on my back while I held him in place, I'd crouch down to the floor so he could just walk off my back to the floor without hurting his legs.

He always found a way of letting me know if he wanted my back so he could do it himself or if he wanted to be carried in my arms. He loved being cradled on his back staring into my eyes as I gently rocked him.

This particular evening though Oreo had his nap in the shelves and when he called for me I came back and offered him my back as always. Oreo decided to jump off my back to the floor instead of to the bed as normal. He misjudged his jump and hit his rear leg on the laundry basket. He let out the worst squeal I ever heard. He tried to get up but couldn't walk. I quickly picked him up and off to emergency we went.

Oreo was crying in the car the whole way to emergency, so I sang to him to try to calm him. Oreo regained some movement in his leg by the time we reached the hospital, but was still limping very badly.

Oreo dislocated his knee. He once again needed surgery, but with his history of seizures and complications he was not a candidate. We increased his pain medicine and within days Oreo regained his full mobility and returned to his busy active lifestyle.

Oreo had a rough few years since surgery, with the seizures and rolling skin, losing his tooth, and dislocating his knee. Through it all Oreo remained my faithful, loyal, loving baby boy while exercising great courage and proving that love truly does conquer all.

Chapter 19

Heaven Bound

Aug. 4'15 started off as a regular day. I awoke to Oreo's grooming and his gentle tap on my mouth and we raced down the stairs to get our morning started. As the morning progressed, Oreo was showing signs of constipation. I thought he just needed to work through it and left for work.

I couldn't believe my eyes when I walked back into my house. Oreo was laying at the front door, covered in feces, urine and blood and was very weak. Alley was sitting close by keeping him company. I'm certain that she was filling in for me to remind him to "Just Purr."

I quickly investigated the house to try to figure out what happened as I called the vet. There were dime size droplets throughout the entire house, except in my bedroom. After getting off the phone with the receptionist at my regular clinic I rushed Oreo to emergency.

The vet came in with his x-rays; one kidney was only an eighth of the size it should be and the other was three times the size it should be. As I looked at the x-rays I was in shock and thought "This can't be happening. Not to Oreo." She continued telling me that Oreo has kidney disease and is in failure.

"Does that mean it's time to?" I asked and thankfully she stopped me before I had to finish my question. "No", she said. "Look at him. Look at his eyes, there is so much life left in them and he loves you so much. He's not ready yet, either." She continued telling me that he is extremely dehydrated and needs IV fluids, which means he will need to stay in the hospital for a few days.

She proceeded to tell me about his continued care with sub-q fluids at home. With treatment most cats do quite well and live many more months or even years. With that I agreed to leave Oreo at the hospital for treatment.

I was anxious as I haven't been away from Oreo for more than a regular work day in over three years. I was worried he may get separation anxiety so I brought him one of my old sweaters and his favorite toy to have in his kennel.

I visited him every morning before work and every evening after work. He would get so excited to see me by the next evening he was eating treats out of my hand. By the second morning the assistant brought Oreo to me and mentioned that after I left the night before he ate a little bit of food and seemed to be doing better. Oreo was so excited to see me he came running to me and curled into my lap, and just as quickly jumped out of my lap and started to dig in my purse looking for his treats. I gave him a few, and shortly after as I was getting ready to leave for work Oreo had another seizure. The first epileptic type since he lost his tooth in 2011. I was in shock and cried for help.

The vet came in and said "It was just too much excitement for him. He has separation anxiety and all though he should probably

stay one more day; he is likely to recover better at home with you."
Oreo was released at 8:00pm Aug 6'15.

We left the hospital with four new medicines to figure out, but
halleluiah my precious Oreo was coming home! Oreo was so happy
when we got home, he ran around the house searching every room.
Alley was also relieved to see him, the couple of days he was in the
hospital she was wandering the house meowing frantically looking
for him. They greeted each other with rubs and gentle love bites, and
Oreo continued running through the house till he came running to
me for cuddles.

Watching Oreo that evening I realized that when we left the
house Tuesday night he wasn't expecting he'd make it back home.
Alley and I were sure thankful that he did. Our family wouldn't be
complete without him.

The medicine made Oreo very lethargic and he slept the whole
week. I brought him to our regular clinic every few days for sub-q
fluids while I tried to learn. I was extremely nervous of needles at
the best of times; let alone sticking my baby boy with one.

I was worried of how he would respond to this treatment. I was
very concerned of his physical reactions and if it would cause too
much stress and/or more seizures. I was also concerned of how it
would affect our relationship that has been built on immense trust
and love.

The whole team at crowfoot veterinary loved Oreo. They were
also extremely patient with me and very supportive. Amy, Oreo's
favorite technician and cat sitter, offered to come to my house to
show me how to do it at home. Amy has been such a blessing to
Oreo and I over the years, there are no words to express my gratefulness for her. When Oreo first started getting seizures Amy became
Oreo's cat sitter, which gave me great peace while I was away. I knew

Oreo and Alley were in good hands with Amy checking in on them and giving them some TLC.

Amy was so kind and gentle with Oreo. Since he came home from the hospital he liked to lay in a cardboard box, so we administered the sub-q while Oreo was in his box. After Amy left, Oreo had a sensitivity seizure and for the first time in fifteen years he ran away from me instead of towards me for comfort.

It broke my heart as I knew Oreo was saying no to this treatment. Without treatment his lifespan will be shorter. I knew his quality of life had to be my main focus and I had to put my feelings aside while I try to do what's right for Oreo.

Dr. Kean was fabulous and assured me the sub-q is not always the right treatment for every cat. Some cats do well, some don't. "Oreo's relationship with you comes first," she said. She recommended trying a calcitriol that can be mixed into his food, with probiotics and vitamin b.

Oreo did quite well on the calcitriol and started acting more normal, but something was different. Oreo was letting Alley have my lap more often and he would sit beside us on the couch. For fifteen years Oreo has always had claim on my lap. I knew he was preparing for the day he would have to leave us. He was instructing Alley to take care of mom when he's gone.

Months went by with Oreo having a few 'mini dehydration crashes' so we'd go to the vet office and let them administer the sub-q fluids. Oreo did ok at the vet office, but would not allow it at home.

By Christmas time I was once again wondering if I was being fair to Oreo. He was everything to me and I loved him so much, but I knew I had to do what was right for him. He started having the sensitivity seizures again almost daily, and was no longer wanting his gabapentin or methamozal that he'd been taking for years.

I called our clinic and made a euthanasia appointment for the 14th of December. I had spent many hours in prayer for Oreo over the years, but my prayers increased drastically upon making the appointment. I prayed that God would give me peace that I was doing right by Oreo. I prayed for a miracle that God would heal him. I pleaded with him to heal him just enough to wait for the rapture. I prayed that God would come and take us all together.

As the dreaded day drew closer I knew I would never be able to forgive myself if I did it too soon. I also knew I'd never forgive myself if I waited too long and he suffered or died while I was at work. Everyone told me that I will know when it's time because Oreo will tell me. His eyes were saying it wasn't time, but his body was telling me that it was. I decided to have him retested to determine how close he was to the end stages.

Miraculously his levels for kidneys seem to have improved. They were better than they were back in August! His calcium levels were higher which could be a sign of cancer, but with him taking calcitriol it could be related to the medicine. I cancelled the appointment and we took him off calcitriol. Within days he started improving.

Oreo and I were blessed with two more wonderful months together before God called him home on February 26, 2016.

A Mother Grieves

(Raw and unedited)
Letters to Oreo

Sunday February 28'16

My Darling Oreo,

There are no words to express my grief over your passing. The months before I hated leaving you to go to work, scared of what would be behind the door when I returned. Feb. 26'16 will be forever engrained in my memory as the worst day of my life.

The second I walked in and turned on the light I glanced at the counter expecting you to be there. You weren't. I went to put my jacket on the bench and turned back to put my stuff in the kitchen, before I went to check on you upstairs. The second I turned back I was relieved to see you on the couch, and then I got closer and saw you drooling excessively. My heart sank as I scolded myself "I shouldn't have gone to work."

Then I put you on the floor to feed you and you fell on your side. "No God No! Not Him!" I screamed. I sat with you for a few minutes letting my tears flow. I knew instantly that dreaded time had come. The time I could no longer put you through any more pain or suffering. I had to love you enough to let you go.

I picked you up and tried to get your kennel out of the closet with you in one arm, but I had to put you down. Your legs were so feeble, but somehow you managed to climb in and lay down. I'm not sure how I drove to the vet, but somehow we made it.

If I could have saved you, you know I would have, just as I know if you could have mustered the strength to stay you would have. Our love for one another isn't up for debate. I know you love me as much as I love you and vice versa.

When the vet came out she said you'd have to stay in the hospital for a few days. I knew watching your last few months you were fighting so hard to stay, but your body was losing the battle. I love you too much to put you through that. I knew I had to love you enough to let you go.

Then they put us in our private room. I hope and pray those last few minutes you felt my love. As I sat with your lifeless body I knew you were no longer in my arms. Jesus squeezed my shoulder as he took you from my arms and into his.

I'm sorry baby that I couldn't sit with you longer; it was just too much to bear. I knew as I cradled your body that you were no longer in pain. You were instantly in the arms of your creator and received a new body, one that works and has no pain.

I long for the day to hold you again and kiss you and tell you how much I love you! I miss you so much my boy, I don't know how I'm going to survive without you.

Feb 29'16

My precious baby boy,

I can't even begin to describe how much I miss you. It's been about 68 hours since you left me, and it's been absolutely horrid!

I can't sleep without you here. I had only 2 hours of sleep Friday night, till Natalie called at 6:30am. We cried and cried, and I was able to get a couple more hours of sleep after our chat.

I came downstairs hoping it was just a horrible dream. I hoped so desperately to see you on the couch or on the counter, but you weren't there. I lost it. I made my coffee and tried to pull myself together and get on with my normal routine, but anything I went to do brought me to tears. You weren't there.

When I went to the bathroom you weren't in my lap. Having a shower, you weren't in the tub trying to drink or climbing up my towel when I got out. I picked up your food dishes, and only laid Alley's down. I filled the dishwasher and still can't bear the thought of washing your paw prints off the counter. Three days later, I still can't wash the counter.

I picked up my laundry and you weren't there to jump on my back or into the basket. I tried to make the beds, but you weren't there to roll around in the sheets. I sat down on the couch and you weren't there to comfort me. Coming down the stairs you weren't there racing me down or waiting for me at the bottom to carry you up.

I left for work today and you weren't there to jump on my back as I put on my shoes or leaping into my arms as I reached for my purse. You aren't here for me to read you your bedtime stories. You're not here to put me to sleep with your purrs, or to lick my fingers after I eat our favorite snacks. You're not here. You are though forever engrained in my heart.

Mar 1'16

Oreo, my precious baby Oreo,

I picked up your ashes today; I can't even begin to describe how painful that was. I love you so much baby boy, and I know I always will.

I picked out a necklace vile to keep you close to my heart. It has paw prints. I debated between paws, hearts and the word love, but paws say it all. Your paw prints are stamped all over my heart.

With that realization I was able to come home and muster the strength to wash your dirty paw prints off the counter, after I made you a beautiful resting place. You were the heart of the home, its only right to keep you there. I've made you a resting place in the china cabinet overlooking the main floor, right beside mommy's couch. I need you close to me, but safe from Alley's curious and clumsy ways.

You always wanted in the china cabinet when I dusted. I guess you found a way to get in.

Friday, March 4'16

Oreo my love,

One week today I woke up to you sitting on the couch just waiting for me to come downstairs. After a few cuddles I made my coffee, but you just wanted to stay on the couch while I continued my morning routine.

Oh how I wish I could turn back time. How I wish I would have skipped work and stayed home with you. I planned on taking you to the vet on Saturday for more fluids. I knew you weren't feeling well, I should have stayed with you. I'm sorry baby boy, I'm so sorry!

When I got home and saw you on the couch, I wish I sat with you longer. I was in denial, you can't be that sick. I wanted to feed you, and then you fell on your side. I screamed "No God No! Not Him!"

When we got to emergency, I held you while I sang to you, "You are going to see the king, no more dying there, you are going to see the king." I haven't a clue how that song came into my mind or how I even uttered the words.

The vet came in and started to prepare your final injection. I cried "I'm sorry. I'm sorry. I'm sorry." I'm sorry is all I could say as you slipped away. I wish so badly I could have uttered one more time, I love you baby boy. However I also know my love, you knew beyond a shadow of a doubt you were loved beyond measure.

I'm sorry Oreo my love couldn't save you. I'm sorry I went to work. I'm sorry you had to endure so much in your short life.

This past week has been awful without you. I always dreaded the day when God would take you to your eternal home. I prayed he'd take us together in the rapture. When I had you retested back in Dec and cancelled the dreaded appointment for the 14th, I thought God was answering my request. He gave us two more wonderful months together before he called you home.

I didn't think I'd be able to survive without you. You are my comfort and my joy. You were my reason for living. You were my motivation. Back in 2009 when I couldn't afford your surgery, I vowed that I will never again be in a position where I couldn't provide for your needs. I quit my real estate career right then and there, and went back to work for my parents to earn a regular pay cheque. It's hard to believe that in only a few short years I managed to get out of debt, do renovations, buy the Camaro and put tens of thousands into your care and medical bills. Only by the grace of God was that possible.

As I started writing your book, I see that God has had his hands on us right from the very start. He promises to provide and says that every good gift comes from his hand.

Oreo you were my special gift from God. Created by him specifically for me. All the love, comfort and joy you provided throughout our 15 years and 4 months together was a tangible glimpse of God's unfailing love for us.

Thank you Oreo for your love. Thank you for picking me and giving me the honor of being your mom. Thank you for being more than "just a cat", thank you for being my precious baby boy.

When we got the news back in August that you had kidney disease, I knew you had instructed Alley to take care of mom. Not even I could have been prepared for how you trained her to show your love from beyond the grave.

Thank you for loving me so much. You fought so hard to stay. You loved me as much as I loved you and you weren't ready to go. You were on a mission and couldn't leave till Alley was trained to look after mom.

You'd be so proud of her and how she has stepped up to the plate. When I got home from the vet without you, Alley was waiting for me on the ottoman. I scooped her up and buried my head while I cried into her fur. She didn't fuss or demand her food, even though I know she was hungry. In fact one week later she hasn't demanded anything.

She sits with me from the time I get home till the time I go to bed. She misses you too. She still waits for you at bedtime and guards your side of the bed. She nestles into your blanket on the couch. She goes to your treat tray and whimpers as she eats a few treats for you. Her whiny meow has turned into a cry. Her heart is also broken.

I promise you Oreo, I will find a way to carry on. Alley needs me. I will pour my love into Alley as I always have. I won't close my heart.

You I know are alive and well in heaven. I know I will see you again and get to hug you and kiss you and tell you how much I love you. I can't wait till you take a flying leap into my arms, when we meet at heaven's gate.

There have been so many days where I have wanted to beg God to send you back. He keeps reminding me where you are, and to wish for you back would be selfish and wouldn't be fair to you.

You are having the time of your life and don't even realize mommy isn't there. I know you are healed and have a new body, one that works and has no pain. You are running in heaven's green pastures, smelling all the pretty flowers and eating the grass freely, without mommy tugging on your leash. You are free to climb the trees and chase the butterflies.

When I look at your memorial I set up, I am reminded that I have your earthly remains, but God has you safely guarded under the shadow of his wings.

I know you loved me beyond measure and you brought me so much joy, comfort and love. You never brought me pain in your life, so I know you would not want me to think of you and remember only the pain that came with your passing. You would want me to remember all our countless happy moments.

As a memory came back I wrote it down. I spent all day Sunday writing to you, about you and our special memories. Before I knew it I had enough for six chapters in your book. Not necessarily in order, but certainly a good start. By the end of the week I almost have your book written, I miss you so much I don't know what to do without you, so I write. As I write I cry and I laugh. I cry because I miss you, I laugh because you brought so much joy.

Oreo I need you to know, the pain I feel is the worse pain imaginable. They say there is nothing worse than a mother losing a child; I know how deep that pain is now. There is only one way I am able to pull myself out of bed and continue putting one foot in front of the other. His name is Jesus.

From the time I called mom and dad (grandma and grandpa) a prayer chain had been started. I can feel those prayers Oreo. I know that God has me in one arm and you in the other. I take comfort in the fact that we will be together again.

God has said he has made a plan for his children and the animals. There are many verses about animals in heaven. God's faithfulness is evident as I write your story. I am reminded that God gives us the desires of our heart and he desires to lavish his love on us. If he could love me so much in this life to give me you, I know he loves me enough to give you back for all eternity.

I long for the day when God wipes every tear from our eyes and takes away all the pain we have suffered on this earth. I press on because my life is worth living because Christ died for us so that we may have life.

I have to surrender you to God and trust in him to bring me through this dark valley. He gives me comfort and he reminds me each and every day of his love for me and all his creation. We serve a risen savior and death was conquered on the cross. Though death may separate us in this life, we are promised an eternal life in glory with God our father.

God has promised that all things work together for good for those who love God, according to his purpose. I know God has a purpose and he can use your passing to restore my soul.

I love you more than words can say Oreo and I can't wait to see you again. Till we meet again enjoy your brothers and sisters and cousins. Tell them all I love them too. Most of all baby boy enjoy your new home, you've earned it!

All my love,

Mommy

A Poem for Oreo

Written by Caralee Jardine
(aka) Mommy

I've placed your picture by my bed
I need to see you to rest my head.
I miss the rhythm of your purr
To sleep without there's no cure,
I miss the feel of your soft fur
How to live without you I'm not sure.
I search for a sign in the sky
Oh how I wish I could fly,
To bring you back, but that wouldn't be right
You've been healed and have new sight.
You're in the fields of heaven
Chasing birds to your delight,
My time will come, just you wait
And there you'll be at heaven's gate!

Though death may separate, no memory can depart.
For in my heart you'll always be, forever with me.

OREO JARDINE
Forever Loved, Forever Cherished
Adopted Oct 18'00-Feb 26'16

Though death may separate in this life, forever we are joined in
our hearts, soul and mind. I rest in the promise of our reunion
in heaven when all creation bows down to Jesus proclaiming

"Worthy is the Lamb…"

Till we meet again my darling boy, mommy loves
you now and for all eternity! Rip my love.

References

God cares for animals:

- Genesis 1:21-26 (God created animals first for his enjoyment)
- Genesis 1:28 (God gave human dominion over animals, did not relinquish ownership)
- Genesis 6:19 (Spared animals from the flood and included animals in the covenant)
- Job 38:41 (Provides for animals)
- Psalm 50:10-11 (God's ownership of animals)
- Psalm 147:9 (provision)
- Proverbs 12:10 (cares about treatment of animals)
- Matthew 10:29-31 (not even a sparrow can die without God knowing and caring)
- James 3:7 (all animals are tame, and hear God's voice)

Animals are in tune with God and Spiritual forces:
- Job 12:7-10, Job 35:11 (animals can teach us)
- Numbers 22:21-41 (Donkey sees angel and speaks)
- Jonah 1:17 & Jonah 2:10 (God commanded whale and whale obeyed)

Animals have souls and spirits:
- Genesis 1:30
- Genesis 7:15 (breath of life)
- Job 12:10 (every living thing has a soul and is in God's hand)
- Psalm 150:6
- Ecclesiastes 3:19-20 (man has no advantage over animal, who are we to say who goes up and who goes down whether man or beast.)

Animals are also in heaven with God's elect:
- Psalms 36:6
- Ecclesiastes 12:7, 3:20
- Isaiah 11:6-9
- Luke 3:6 (All flesh shall see salvation of God)
- John 14:2-6 (Jesus is the way to heaven)
- Romans 8:19-23 (animals also wait for redemption and are delivered along with the children of God)
- 1Corinthians 15:42-44, 52-55
- 1 Thessalonians 4:13-18, 5:9-11
- Revelation 4:6-11, 5:11-13, 19:11, 21:5 (animals praise Jesus in heaven where ALL things are made new)

Verses for comfort and peace:

- Psalm 23 & 36:7, 37:45, 46:1-2, 46:10
- Ecclesiastes 9:4
- Isaiah 40:31, 41:10
- Jeremiah 29:11
- Matthew 6:25-26, 33-34, 11:28-29
- John 3:1, 16-17, 10:27-29, 14:1, 27
- Romans 5:8, 8:28
- 2Corinthians 5:8
- Philippians 4:6-7
- 1Peter 5:7

Additional references: www.fathersloveletter.com & Jack Van Impe: Animals in Heaven

God's answers to my questions and doubt.

Who picked you up off the floor and who drove you to the vet?

Who uttered the words for you that you could not?

Why would I touch your shoulder, if I wasn't there to receive him? Do I give false peace?

The peace that passes all understanding comes from whom? At your lowest points you trusted me that I have Oreo. Keep your trust in me and my words, and the peace and comfort I have given you. Lean not on man's misunderstanding or misinterpretation of my words.

Who put the song "You're going to see the king" into your head and all the hymns you sang as a child?

The week before, Oreo and you watched the Lazarus movie and the 1st time in 40yrs instead of being fixed on the miracle you felt sorry for Lazarus being ripped out of heaven.

I know how much you love Oreo, and I know the grief is more than you could bear. If your parents were home, you would lean on them instead of me. Human strength will not get you through this. You require the strength that only I can give you. I am all you need. Lean on me.

Who took the decision out of your hand and gave you peace of my divine appointment? I knew you could not live with the guilt of making that decision. I gave you 2 more months to prepare you, now you need to trust me that he slept all day till you got home. Remember when Oreo's seizures happened? He waited for you.

The bible was written for man, not animals. Man sinned; not animals. As much as you love Oreo, I assure you I love him more. He is my gift to you, but he is mine. I have made a plan for man and animals. When you are absent from the body, you are present with the Lord. You live by faith not by sight.

When in doubt remember my love for you. I sent my son to die for you. If your earthly father knows how to give good gifts to you, how much more will I? I know you wish for Oreo and all your pets to be in heaven. Delight in me and I will give you the desires of your heart, for it is I who gave you those desires.

Just as I commanded the whale to swallow Jonah, I commanded Oreo to grab your arm all those years ago at the humane society. He is my gift to you. I am a loving God and I desire to lavish my love on you. Oreo is your son, given to you by me. I also know the pain of the death of a child. I sent my son to die for you so you may have life. Death was conquered on the cross. I did not give you a spirit of fear, but of peace and a sound mind. Trust me; Oreo is with me safely guarded under the shadow of my wings.

I am the same yesterday today and forever. I am not distant and angry, but am the complete expression of love. I have plans to prosper you and not to harm you. Plans to give you hope and a future. The bible is not silent on animals in heaven; I have said they are delivered along with the children of God. Romans 8:19-23

CARALEE A. JARDINE was born and raised in Calgary, Alberta. From the time she was born she loved animals. When given a choice between playing with friends or animals, the animals always won. Caralee has been in retail management for the past 25 years and is currently running her parent's business.

CPSIA information can be obtained
at www.ICGtesting.com
Printed in the USA
LVOW05s0717300816
502399LV00003B/3/P